HELLO WORLD!

Greetings in 43 Languages

Manja Stojic

Boxer Books

This book is dedicated to Amineta from Togo and all other children like her who have experienced slavery.

— M.S.

Special thanks to:

Franek Strzeszewski
Modern Language School, King's College London.

Language Centre, School of Oriental and African Studies.

First published in Great Britain in 2009 by Boxer Books Limited.
www.boxerbooks.com

First published in the U.S.A. in 2002 by Scholastic Inc.

A CIP catalogue record for this book is available from the British Library upon request.

The illustrations were prepared using acrylic paints. The text is set in Clarendon.

ISBN 978-1-906250-62-1

1 3 5 7 9 10 8 6 4 2

Printed in China

All of our papers are sourced from managed forests and renewable resources.

How to Use This Book:

It is simple to learn to say "hello" in many different languages.

The languages featured in this book span the world from west to east – across the continents from the Americas to Australia.

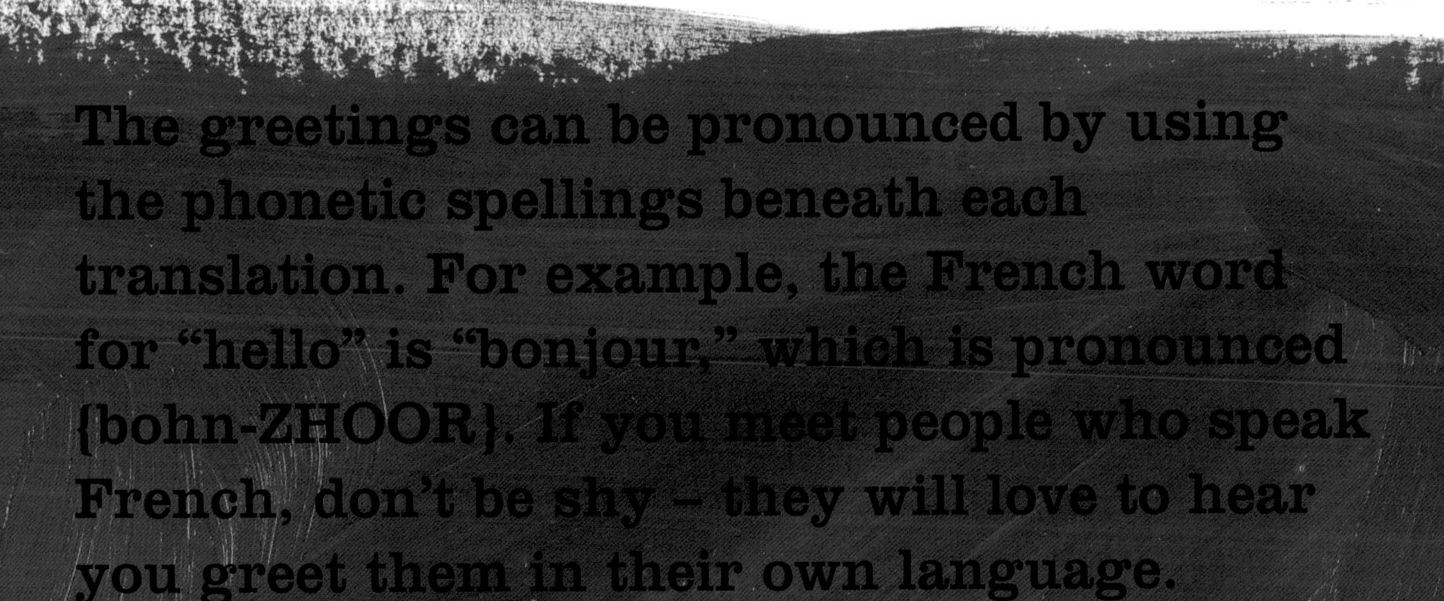

The greetings can be pronounced by using the phonetic spellings beneath each translation. For example, the French word for "hello" is "bonjour," which is pronounced {bohn-ZHOOR}. If you meet people who speak French, don't be shy – they will love to hear you greet them in their own language.

Enjoy saying "hello" in all the languages with your friends and family!

“Hello”

is a very magical word.
Everyone says “hello.”
I hope you will try to
say it in as many
languages as you can.
Pass on the magic
and make people smile!

Aloha!

Hawaiian

{a-LOH-hah}

Kiana!

{kee-AH-nah}

Inuktitut

Buna Ziua!

Romanian {BOO-nuh ZEE-wa}

Hello!

{he-LOH}

English

Cześć!

{CHESHCH}

Polish

Sat Sri Akal!

{Sat SchrEE ikAHI} **Punjabi**

Hylo!

{he-LOH}

Welsh

Olá!

{oh-LAH}

Portuguese

¡Hola!

{OH-lah}

Spanish

Bonjour!

French

{bohn-ZHOOR}

Dutch

Hallo!

{he-LOH}

Danish

Hei!
{HAY}

Finnish

Hei!
{HAY}

Norwegian

Hei!
{HAY}

Swedish

Hej!
{HAY}

German

Guten Tag!

{GOO-ten TAHG}

Ciao!

{CHOW}

Italian

Serbian

Zdravo!

{ZDRAH-voh}

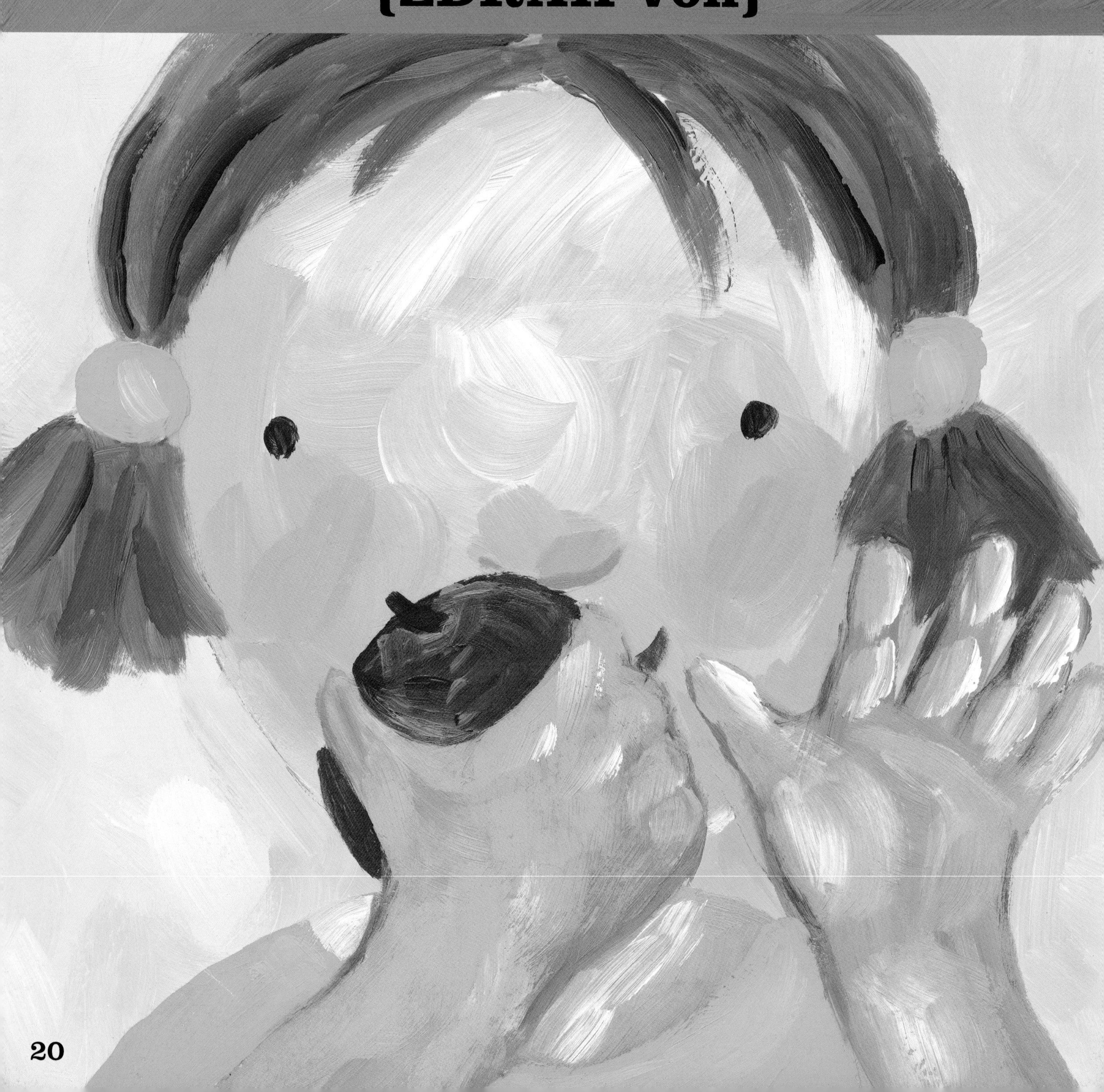

Geia Sou!

{YAH soo}

Greek

Zdravstvuite!

Russian {ZZDRAHST-vet-yah}

Merhaba!

{MER-hah-bah}

Turkish

Shalom!

Hebrew {shah-LOHM}

Salaam!

Arabic

{sah-LAHM}

Amharic

Selam!

{se-LAHM}

Bafia

Wayumbe!

{wah-YOOM-beh}

Bambara

I ni bara!

{ee nee BAH-rah}

Dinka

Ci yi bak!

{see yee BAHK}

Zulu

Sawubona!

{sah-woo-BOH-nah}

Kayira be!

Mandinka {kah-HEE-rah beh}

Jambo!

{JAM-boh}

Swahili

Bengali

Nomoskaar!

{NOH-moh-skahr}

Hindi

Namasté!

{[illegible]-STAY}

Vanakkam!

Tamil

{vah-nah-KUM}

Adaab!

Urdu

{ah-DAHB}

Thai

Vietnamese

Mandarin

Níh hâo!

{nee HAOW}

Korean

Annyoung Hasimnikka!

{an-YOH HAS-him-ni-kah}

Czech

Ahoj!

{AHOY}

Maalin Wanaagsan!

{mAHlin wanAHgsan} Somali

Kia Ora!

Maori {KEE-ah OH-rah}

INDEX

Amharic 26
Arabic 25
Bafia 27
Bambara 27
Bengali 30
Cantonese 33
Czech 36
Danish 17
Dinka 27
Dutch 16
English 9
Finnish 17
French 15
German 18
Greek 21
Hawaiian 6
Hebrew 24
Hindi 30
Inuktitut 7
Italian 19
Japanese 34
Korean 35
Mandarin 33
Mandinka 28
Maori 38
Norwegian 17
Polish 10
Portuguese 13
Punjabi 11
Romanian 8
Russian 22
Serbian 20
Somali 37
Spanish 14
Swahili 29
Swedish 17
Tamil 30
Thai 31
Turkish 23
Urdu 30
Vietnamese 32
Welsh 12
Zulu 27

Hello World!

Manja Stojic was born in Belgrade, Yugoslavia, where she obtained a B.A. degree in graphic design/painting. Since then she has lived in Prague, New York and Harare – all of which have felt like home. Manja now lives in London, England, where she works as a designer, illustrator and writer.

Manja Stojic

{MAN-ya STO-yich}